THE
COURSE

Put six no-hopers in a classroom, add a teacher who is
a conman, stir in a little Positive Mental Attitude and
what do you get? A barrel of laughs, a dash of wisdom
and – eventually – six winners.

"a great show" *Gay Byrne The Late, Late Show*

"this massively funny romp is a winner all the
way. It would be a crime to miss it"
Liverpool Echo

"tears ran down my face with laughter –
brilliant" *Manchester Evening News*

BRENDAN O'CARROLL, well-known as a comedian, is now also acclaimed for his bestselling fiction, *The Mammy*, *The Chisellers* and *The Granny*.

The Course is his first play – not only did he write this box-office hit, he also directed and starred in it. *The Course* had a sell-out tour in Ireland, Britain and the US.

Other Books By Brendan O'Carroll

The Mammy
The Chisellers
The Granny
The Mammy Talking Book

THE
COURSE

A Play
by
Brendan O'Carroll

ⅅ

THE O'BRIEN PRESS
DUBLIN

First published 1996 by The O'Brien Press Ltd.,
20 Victoria Road, Rathgar, Dublin 6, Ireland.

1   2   3   4   5   6   7   8   9   10
96 97 98 99 00 01 02 03 04 05
British Cataloguing-in-Publication Data
A catalogue reference for this title is available from the British Library

ISBN 0-86278-493-X

The O'Brien Press is assisted by The Arts Council/An Chomhairle Ealaíon
The publishers wish to thank Pat Baker for kind permission to reproduce
the photographs that appear in this book.

Cover and inside photographs: Pat Baker
Cover design: The O'Brien Press Ltd.
Typesetting, design, layout: The O'Brien Press Ltd.
Colour separations: Lithoset Ltd., Dublin
Printing: Mackay's of Chatham plc, Kent

ACKNOWLEDGEMENTS

As with every work that I have undertaken, nothing can be achieved alone,
so it is with my most sincere thanks that I acknowledge
the contribution of the following:

Doreen O'Carroll
Colette Mary Browne
Rory Cowan
Shay Fitzsimons
Dermot "Bugsy" O'Neill
John Keegan
David Lang
Stephen O'Halloran
Jimmy Staunton
Alan Kelly
Ashley Browne
Evelyn Conway
Tony Byrne (Tivoli Theatre)
Kelly McErlaine
Jacinta & Mick (Digges Lane)
Tyrone Productions
Kevan Johnson
Canada Life Insurance (Irl)
Shay McGrath
Brian Tracey
Steve Blaunt
Roddy Doyle
Paul Mercier
Andy O'Callaghan
Pat Baker
Mary & Chenile (The O'Brien Press)
My thanks to you all for your hard work, belief and encouragement.

I would also like to give a special mention to three actors
who were not in the original production, but when called upon came through
with magnificently professional performances, each of them enhancing the
production with their presence. They are:

Gerard Lee
Niall Murray
and
Mike Pyatt

This Play is dedicated to my daughter
Fiona
of whom I am so very proud

FOREWORD

I have always believed in the power of a Positive Mental Attitude (PMA). However, PMA alone can achieve little. There are two other ingredients that must accompany it for it to become a "force". They are action and planning.

Action means that if you have the idea and you truly believe it to be a winner, then "do" something about it!!! The world is full of people who thought of something years ago or who could have made millions but did nothing about their idea at the time. Once you begin the action the PMA will keep you going even after you have been rejected, ridiculed and over-run with people telling you that you're wasting your time. No action is a waste of time, provided it is of a positive nature and does not transgress the laws of God or Man. Your PMA will ensure this. In short, action equals hard bloody work!

Planning is simply knowing what you want to achieve at the end of your action. Unless you know this, do not begin! No aircraft would take off without knowing where it was going, this would be a waste of fuel and time, don't waste yours. Know where you are going and you will be surprised at the way the world stands back and makes room for you.

Believe it or not, each of the characters in our play already have two of the three ingredients needed to be a winner. Action is what brought them to "The Course" and they know what they want, they want to sell insurance. So they have a destination; the only factor missing is their PMA.

Joe Daly will not teach them PMA, for it is not something that can be taught. I believe that we are all born with our share of PMA, but over the years from childhood on and even well into adulthood it is suppressed by the many negatives that are heaped upon us in the name of "reality". Do you want some realities? I'll give you some:

Christy Brown became one of Ireland's greatest artists although he only had the use of his left foot.

Eamonn Coghlan ran a sub-four minute mile at forty-one years of age.

How? Because they believed they could and they worked so hard it had to happen!

Let me give you another example. A prisoner on death row for many, many years told his cellmate one day – no not one day, every day – that he would eventually walk out of that prison a free man and not only that but that he would become president of that country. Impossible? That man is Nelson Mandela. You make the reality. You make it happen.

You really are a Child of the Universe, and it belongs to you. The only limits are those you set upon yourself.

Brendan O'Carroll
DUBLIN 1996

INTRODUCTION

The fictional company, Major Accident, is an American-owned insurance company specialising in accident policies. The policy is very cheap – only £30 per year – so to make any kind of money on commission one must sell a lot of policies per day. To enable its sales people to do this the company has devised a two-week course that teaches its prospective representatives "The System".

"The System" is a patter that must be learned word for word and delivered with a positive mental attitude or "PMA". One of the drawbacks of the company's cheap policy is a high turnover of sales staff. As a result there is a permanent recruitment drive on, and "The Course" is always running. The lecturer receives £150 for each pupil who successfully completes "The Course" by passing the final exam. It is precisely because of this payment that few, if any, pupils ever fail.

The company's adverts in the "Wanted" columns begin "Do you want to make £1,000 per week? No experience necessary, etc." This advert attracts the largest collection of losers you could find anywhere. In our play "The Course" we follow six of these applicants from day one to their final exam on the two-week course.

The Characters

Joe Daly *(The lecturer)*

About forty years old, he did at one time consider himself to be an expert in communications. He's been giving the PMA course for Major Accident Insurance for over five years now but of late he has just been passing pupils to get the cash, and is convinced he has "lost it". This particular course is to become a personal test for him.

Burt Rubenstein *(Company Group Controller)*

A thirty-five year old American. The company is unhappy with the standard of pupil being passed out by Daly, so they have sent Burt to sit in on this course to watch him in action and assess his ability. Would love to fire Daly.

The Pupils

Emily Beechmont

Thirty-five to forty years old. Married, Emily is doing "The Course" because her husband Bernard says she should do "something". Middle/upper class, has never worked a day in her life and is completely dominated by Bernard who treats her like she is worthless!

Will Benson

About thirty-five years old. An alcoholic: bitter, cynical, never a good word to say about anyone or anything. A big man with an intimidating manner.

Tina Lovejoy (Clarke)

Between twenty and twenty-five years old; very pretty. Tina is a prostitute. She wants to give it up and believes she will make a super salesperson in the insurance world. Street-wise, with a mouth like a "skanger".

Tony Short

About forty. A bit of a wimp, he has been made redundant from the bus company where he was a stores controller.

Bill Weston

A movie addict, Bill thinks life is a big movie and he behaves as if he is the star. He is dapper, well-spoken and an entertainer. Always has a funny quip and looks to be the man most likely to succeed on "The Course".

Ben Wilson

About thirty years old. Ben has always been told he is as thick as a plank. He has never had a job for more than one week and was always sacked because of some huge disaster he caused.

The Course was first staged at the Tivoli Theatre, Dublin on 9 October 1995.

THE CAST

Joe Daly: Brendan O'Carroll
Emily Beechmont: Jennifer Gibney
Will Benson: Gerry Browne
Tina Lovejoy: Esther Doorley
Tony Short: Ciaran McMahon
Ben Wilson: Brendan Morrissey
Burt Rubenstein: Paul Lee
Bill Weston: Brendan Kealy

THE PRODUCTION TEAM

Director : Brendan O'Carroll
Assistant Director: Brendan Morrissey
Producers: Gerry Browne & Tommy Swarbrigg
Designers: Fiona Whelan & Fiona Leech
Wardrobe Designer: Mary Cullen
Production Supervisor: Shay Fitzsimons
Lighting: Andrew Leonard

ACT ONE

Scene One

[The stage is dark. In the centre back a screen comes alive. During the play a number of slides are projected onto it. The slides are white print on black. Slide 1 reads: "The Course by Brendan O'Carroll."

The theme music, a romanticised version of "Graduation Day", the closing tune, plays. As music fades, the lights come up and Slide 2 reads: "A hotel somewhere in Ireland."

The scene is a small conference room in a hotel somewhere in Ireland. JOE DALY is standing in the doorway, leaving his class. They have just finished their course and all have passed the final exam. JOE DALY is in full flight, wrapping up the class.]

JOE: *[to backstage]* Well done, all of you. You have no idea how unusual it is for everyone to pass this course. Good luck on Monday!

[JOE closes the door and turns to audience with a smile on his face. It suddenly changes to a scowl.]

JOE: Fuck!

[JOE begins to tidy up the bits and pieces the pupils have left on the conference table. The phone rings on the desk. JOE walks to the desk and picks up the telephone.]

JOE: Hello, Major Accident Sales Course. Joe Daly speaking. Can I help you?

[There is a pause. JOE sits in his chair and puts his feet up on the desk.]

JOE: Ah, Deirdre. Hello, darling ... yes, just finished. *[pause]* What? Yes, they all passed ... of course they did. *[JOE laughs, then there is a pause]* No, they weren't any good. *[Once again JOE laughs, another pause]* Deirdre, darling, if they were any good they wouldn't have been here in the first place. It's the nature of the business. It attracts losers who think they will become millionaires overnight by selling insurance. *[pause]* Yes ... well, that was when I was starting off, dear. I had the enthusiasm then, now it's just a job. *[pause]* Oh, I don't know, Deirdre darling. Perhaps PMA just isn't as relevant today as it used to be. In any case I had five more passed out today, so I get my

£150 per pupil passed, that's all that matters. *[pause]* It's just a job, dear, just a job.

[A well-dressed man enters in background. JOE *spots him.]*

JOE: I have to go, Deirdre, I have to go. *[whispers]* I love you too.

[JOE hangs up the phone. The man is browsing through some papers left on the table. JOE *rises to greet him. He does not know who this man is, but has a feeling this is not good.]*

JOE: Yes?

BURT: Mr Joe Daly?

JOE: That's correct ...

BURT: My name is Burt Rubenstein. As you may know I am the group controller for Major Accident.

JOE: Indeed I do, you're most welcome, Mr Rubenstein, most welcome, indeed. What brings you to my little corner of the company's affairs?

BURT: Frankly, Mr Daly, I'm here on a fact-finding mission. Could you close the door just for a moment so we can talk?

JOE: Fact-finding mission?

[JOE closes door.]

19

BURT: Take a seat, Mr Daly.

[*JOE sits uneasily.*]

BURT: Mr Daly, I've been sent here from head office.

JOE: In the Cayman Islands?

BURT: Well, no, that's just our registered office. Our head office is actually in Chicago. Now, as I was saying, I've been sent here because sales in the emerald area, which is what we call Ireland, are worse than they have ever been.

JOE: [*standing*] Well, I have some ideas ...

BURT: I'm sure you do, sit down, Mr Daly. Now, I have already done an intensive study of our sales people in the field and I've come across quite a few that have graduated from your class here, Mr Daly.

JOE: [*pleased*] Oh! And how are they?

BURT: In the United States we would call them "bums".

JOE: Oh. Would you?

BURT: They don't use our sales system, in fact, they don't seem to know what the system is. Now, perhaps they were clever enough to convince you in their graduation exam that they were good enough to go into the field. Or else they're very stupid, in which case they should never have been put in the field, and you, Mr Daly, would not have been collecting your $200 per pupil passed under false pretences.

JOE: *[indignantly]* I resent that accusation!

BURT: Sit down, Mr Daly. For now let's call it an allegation, and that's the reason I'm here: I'm here to prove myself wrong.

JOE: And how do you intend to do that, Mr Rubenstein?

BURT: Well, from Monday I will join your new class and, for the next two weeks, I will watch exactly how you present the system, how you train the pupils. Only this time, Mr Daly, *I* will mark the graduation exam papers.

[JOE jumps up, startled.]

JOE: But, I always mark those papers. Why would you do that?

[BURT takes JOE by the arm and leads him stage front.]

BURT: You prove me wrong, Mr Daly, and I'm out of here. But if you can't get at least a seventy percent success rate with this class you've got, then, Mr Daly, *you're* out of here.

JOE: Seventy percent?

BURT: That's correct, Mr Daly: seventy percent.

This is the average pass rate for Mainland Europe and the United States. This shouldn't concern you too much as, looking back on your record, I note that you have a very high percentage of passes. In fact, in the last two years nobody has ever failed in your class. Now that, sir, is an extraordinary record and one which I will be privileged to witness right here in this classroom over the next fortnight!

JOE: And how am I to explain your sitting in on the class to the pupils?

BURT: I think it would be appropriate if you introduced me to the class as somebody involved in sales in the field team. Let's say here for a refresher course.

JOE: A refresher course?

BURT: A refresher course.

JOE: Seventy percent?

BURT: Seventy percent.

[JOE ponders this for a moment.]

BURT: Ok, so, I'm out of here. Mr Daly, I'll look forward to seeing you here Monday.

[JOE walks BURT to the door.]

JOE: And I look forward to seeing you, Mr Rubenstein. It will be an interesting fortnight and I relish the opportunity of displaying my teaching talents to someone as knowledgable about the business as you are.

BURT: That's very kind of you, Joe, and I look forward to seeing you too in action.

[BURT leaves, JOE closes the door.]

JOE: Wanker.

[JOE rushes to the desk and picks up the telephone and keys in a number.]

JOE: Hello, Monica? It's Joe Daly. *[pause]* I'm fine. How are things at head office? ... Cutbacks? ... Wholesale sackings? *[pause]* Monica, could you put me through to Sandra? Thank you. Love you too, miss you already. *[pause]* Hello, Sandra! Joe Daly ... wonderful, yes, I was just talking to her. Oh, a bitch. Sandra, tell me how many have I got for next week? *[pause]* Six! And tell me, Sandra, have you met them? *[pause]* Good. What are they like, Sandra? *[pause]* Alcoholic? ... A prostitute! *[pause]* Curly, Larry and Moe. No. *[laughs]* Oh, the three Stoog ... *[realises]* The fucking three Stooges. *[sits]* No, not at all, I'm looking forward to the challenge ... thanks very much, Sandra. What? *[pause]* Yes, I'll, eh, see you in three weeks at the annual dinner. Goodbye, Sandra.

[JOE replaces the receiver, picks up his papers and

walks slowly to the door. Turning, he speaks to the telephone.]

JOE: Annual dinner? Unless my pupils next week are six of the Magnificent Seven, in a fortnight's time I won't have any fuckin' dinner.

[Exits.]

Scene Two

[The same meeting room in a hotel. There is a long table with five of our six pupils sitting at it, facing the audience. There is a flip chart, a desk, a chair, and a telephone on the desk. Slide 3 reads: "Day One: The Magnificent Six." The pupils are strangers to each other so there is no conversation. The door opens and a head sticks in. It is BILL

WESTON. *All heads turn to the door.]*

BILL: Is this "The Course"?

[The reply comes from an unshaven man with tossed hair, dressed in a crumpled suit.]

WILL: No. It's a fuckin' Pink Floyd concert.

EMILY: *[rising from seat]* Oh dear! I thought it was "The Course" too!

WILL: It is, love, that was a joke, sit down.

[EMILY sits unsure. BILL takes the vacant seat between WILL and BEN. He turns to BEN and offers his outstretched hand.]

BILL: Hello, my name is Bill Weston!

BEN: That's very like my name!

BILL: Is it? What's your name?

[BEN takes BILL's hand]

BEN: Ben!

BILL: *[stares at BEN for a moment]* Yes ... indeed!

[The room returns to silence. Suddenly the door bursts open and in breezes JOE DALY. Everybody jumps.]

JOE: Good morning!

WILL: Good fuck!

JOE: Good morning, everybody. My, my, what a handsome bunch they have sent me this time. Welcome, welcome, indeed welcome to the first step in changing your life, for today you leave behind the old you and in two weeks' time you will greet the new you!

[JOE walks to the desk and places the bundle of files he is carrying on the desk. He turns and claps his hands.]

JOE: All right, let's get started. Everybody stand up. Come on. Push your chair back and stand. Come along, everybody.

[They all stand sheepishly.]

JOE: Ok! Here we go. It's a long way to Tipperary – come on – it's a long way to go. Everybody, loud, top of your voices.

[EMILY smiles and joins in with enthusiasm as does BILL. TINA is half-hearted, so is TONY. BEN just stands open-mouthed while WILL begins shyly, but increases in volume after a bit.]

JOE: Now ... march on the spot. Come on!

[Everybody marches on the spot. EMILY like a general. The ensemble brings the verse to a close.]

JOE: Ok, ok. That's it. That will do! Sit down again. Now, doesn't everybody feel better?

[BEN *raises his hand.*]

JOE: Yes?

BEN: I don't know the words, sir.

JOE: Sorry?

BEN: I don't know the words! Will you write them out for me?

JOE: You don't need to know them. Just hum along, ok?

BEN: Ok.

JOE: All right, now in front of you you will find a name card upon which I want you to write your first names only. [*turns*] While we're doing that why don't we all introduce ourselves?

[*The class begins to exchange handshakes and introductions loudly.*]

JOE: Stop! No, you introduce yourselves to me.

[*Order returns.*]

JOE: [*with roll book open*] My name is Joe Daly and I will be your course director for the next two weeks. Now perhaps you will give me your full name and the last position of employment you have held. [*points to* TINA] You, dear.

TINA: Tina Lovejoy. Personal entertainer, self-employed.

[WILL *lets out a "ha!". * TINA *gives him the bad eye.*]

EMILY: Emily Beechmont. Home-maker and wife to Bernard.

TONY: Tony Short. Stores manager, transport company.

BEN: Ben Wilson. Part-time counterhand in "The Flamin' Dragon".

WILL: Will Benson. Security guard, "Nookie Nappies".

BILL: Bill Weston. War correspondent, *Catholic Standard.*

[*They all turn slowly to stare at* BILL. *He smiles back confidently.*]

JOE: Good! *[closes book]*

[*They all write names on their respective name cards and place them in front of them. * BEN's *is written in Chinese.*]

JOE: Sorry, eh ... Em, what's that? *[pointing at* BEN's *name card]*

BEN: *[proudly]* It's Chinese. I know a little bit, yeh know.

JOE: Well, unfortunately Ben, I don't know any, so could you please write it in English?

[BEN *flips over the card where his name is written in English.* JOE *walks to the flip chart and writes the letters PMA on the chart. He then turns to his class.*]

JOE: PMA [*slow and deliberate*] P ... M ... A ... Who knows what PMA is?

[TONY *raises his hand.*]

JOE: Ah good man, Tony?

TONY: [*embarrassed*] It's something women get just before a period.

[JOE *stares at* TONY *for a moment, as do all the other members of the cast.* BILL *laughs heartily.*]

BEN: You, eejit. That's not it at all. They get pimples.

TINA: Not all the time, sometimes I do and sometimes I don't.

EMILY: When I was younger I got pimples. Now I just seem to get tired very easily.

WILL: Holy Jaysus. Is this the kind of shite we're going to be talking about for two weeks?

JOE: Hold it, hold it everybody! Let's get this straight from the start: you address all your answers to me. This is not a debating society. The answer I was looking for was Positive Mental Attitude! That's the kind of shi– That's what we

29

will be talking about for the next two weeks.

[BILL raises his hand.]

JOE: Yes ... em, Bill, isn't it?

BILL: Yes, it is indeed, Bill. I would just like to say that in fairness that was a terribly good stab by Tony. PMA and PMT are very close and I think he deserves some kind of recognition for making the effort.

JOE: Absolutely right, Bill, and I'm glad you brought that up, because that's what PMA is all about: turning negatives to positives. You're quite right. Tony, well done: a great effort. Everybody, a little clap for Tony.

[Everybody applauds. TONY hangs his head sheepishly. JOE moves to the flip chart and turns over a page. The words "ENTHUSIASM", "NEED", "CAROLINA NOD" are listed.]

JOE: The PMA we use in selling has three ingredients. *[counts on his fingers]* They are Enthusiasm, Need and lastly, the Carolina Nod. Let's look at them one at a time.

[JOE returns to the flip chart and points to the top word. Turns back to the class.]

JOE: Enthusiasm. Let me hear you say that: "enthusiasm".

GROUP: *[lacklustre]* Enthusiasm.

JOE: No, no. You have to say it enthusiastically, "ENTHUSIASM".

GROUP: *[slightly more enthusiastic]* Enthusiasm.

JOE: Give me an "E".

GROUP: E.

JOE: No, no ... louder. Give me an "E".

GROUP: E.

JOE: Give me an "N".

GROUP: N.

JOE: Give me a "tusi".

GROUP: Tusi.

WILL: Fuckin' tusi.

JOE: Give me an "isim".

GROUP: Isim.

JOE: Put them together, what do yeh get?

GROUP: E ... N ... TUSI ... ISIM.

JOE: Well done, everybody.

> *[The phone on* JOE's *desk rings. He walks to it and picks it up.]*

JOE: Excuse me, everybody. *[speaking into the telephone]* Hello ... Yes ... Well, just one second. Emily Beechmont?

31

[EMILY *looks up surprised and puts her hand in the air.*]

EMILY: Eh, that's me.

JOE: Telephone call.

[EMILY *gets up and hurries to the telephone.*]

EMILY: Oh dear, I hope there's nothing wrong at home.

JOE: Yes ... We all do.

[EMILY *picks up the phone.*]

EMILY: Hello ... Yes, Bernard ... Your golf shoes? They're in the brown press just below the stairs and your five iron is in the kitchen beside the fridge. I got the new grip put on it and picked it up yesterday ... What? The course, oh yes, it's fine, really good ... Ok, dear, bye bye ... Love you too, bye.

[As EMILY *replaces the receiver and walks embarrassed back to her seat,* BURT *enters the room.* EMILY *takes her seat and looks at* JOE.]

EMILY: I'm terribly sorry. Minor emergency.

JOE: That's ok, Emily. Now, allow me to introduce you to the gentleman who has just joined us in the class. This is Mr Burt Rubenstein. Mr Rubenstein is from the sales in the field team, and indeed his sales record is quite impressive. *[He nods to* BURT *and* BURT *nods back.]* However, he will be joining us here in the class for the next two weeks as part of a refresher course. Mr Rubenstein is from the United States of America and I'm sure he would be glad to answer any questions you might have.

[BURT *gestures his acceptance of this.*]

JOE: So does anyone have a question for Mr Rubenstein?

[BEN *and* BILL *prod the shy* TONY *into standing.*]

JOE: Ah, good man, Tony.

[TONY *realises he is trapped into asking a question so he searches and comes up with the obvious.*]

TONY: Where in America are you from, Mr Rubenstein?

BURT: I'm from a place called Hackensack, New Jersey.

[TONY *sits down. Without being announced or asked to,* BEN *shouts out a question.*]

BEN: Do they have a Chinese there?

BURT: I beg your pardon?

[BEN stands and proudly goes on.]

BEN: Do they have a Chinese take-away there in Happensapin, New Jersey?

[JOE stares at BEN aghast.]

JOE: *[aside to Ben]* Sit the fuck down, will you?

BURT: Yes, we have many restaurants from many different cultures and Chinese is indeed among them.

TINA: Are you married?

WILL: Ha, ha ... You're fucked now, Burty.

[BURT seems a little uneasy. He loosens his collar and sits up.]

BURT: Em, divorced actually.

JOE: *[exasperated]* Does anybody have a question relating to Major Accident and sales in the field? That's what I meant.

BILL: I have a question for Mr Rubenstein.

JOE: Eh, yes, Bill. Go ahead.

[BILL slowly rises and throws his pencil onto the desk. As he walks around the table he looks squarely at BURT. He stands and clasps his hands behind his back.]

BILL: Mr Rubenstein ... In your own words tell the

court what you saw on the night of the 24th.

[*Everybody stares in silence for a moment, then the pupils begin to laugh and clap.*]

JOE: [*screaming*] Silence!

[*Everybody stops laughing abruptly.*]

JOE: What do you think you are doing?

BILL: I sensed a bit of tension. I thought a little bit of levity was called for. What do you think?

JOE: Please sit, Bill.

[*JOE now calms down and speaks slowly.*]

JOE: Right. Well, now that the fun and games are over, let's get down to business. Don't get me wrong: a little bit of hilarity is always good and it lightens the heart, but in its place. Let's keep it in its place. [*pause*] Now where were we? ... Yes, how do you become enthusiastic? It's easy to be enthusiastic about something we like, things we like doing. But how do you become enthusiastic when you are doing something you don't particularly like, when you don't feel enthusiastic ... Tina?

[*TINA is a little startled at being chosen.*]

TINA: Well ... When I'm entertaining a client, and let's say I don't particularly like him – maybe he's a dog or somethin' – then I pretend he's Hugh

Grant *[or topical]* and that makes my job a whole lot easier.

JOE: Good, Tina. That's exactly how you do it, when you don't feel enthusiastic you act enthusiastic. If you don't like something, try and think of something positive to say about it. If you don't like someone try and think positive and say something positive about them. Let me give you an example: you give me a negi and I'll give you a posi.

BEN: Czechoslovakian cars are crap.

JOE: Czechoslovakian cars are cheap and even though I'm on a low wage I can afford to buy one. See what I mean? Emily, give me a negi.

EMILY: Cooking is a thankless chore.

JOE: Cooking gives you the opportunity to be creative and expressive. You see, any negative can be turned to a positive: that takes enthusiasm. We will begin and end each session throughout this course with a posi and negi session. You've already had your posi session when we all got up and sang "It's a Long Way to Tipperary". Everybody felt better after that, isn't that right? That builds enthusiasm.

WILL: It was stupid. "It's a Long Way to Tipperary" ... We all looked like gobshites.

BEN: It made me feel good.

WILL: You looked like the biggest gobshite.

BILL: *[in John Wayne voice]* Those are mighty strong words, partner. I hope your gun is as fast as your mouth.

WILL: See what I mean? This fellow is a fuckin' lunatic. Everything he says is out of the movies and he's a blatant liar. War correspondent for the *Catholic Standard* – who ever heard such shite?

BILL: What would you like me to say, chief?

WILL: Just tell the truth.

BILL: The truth ... ha!

WILL: *[now more forceful]* Just tell the truth!

BILL: You want the truth?

WILL: *[louder]* Tell the truth.

BILL: *[in Jack Nicholson voice]* You can't handle the truth.

WILL: See? There he fuckin' goes again.

JOE: Calm down. Calm down, you two, please calm down. Now look, Will, I don't have to remind you that everyone here is attending this course for their own reasons. Am I right? Look at me, Will, am I right?

   [WILL looks up reluctantly.]

WILL: Yeh.

JOE: And each of us will have to accept that we're individuals governed by the influences that we have previously had in our lives. That's the whole point of this course: I am going to present to you the opportunity to take control of your own lives, even you, Will. You may not be here because you want to be but by the end of this course you too, I hope, will have taken control of your own life.

WILL: Yeah, yeah, yeah. But don't make me look stupid.

BILL: Stupid is as stupid does, Mama says.

JOE: Bill, shut the fuck up, will you? *[he gathers himself]* I'm sorry, Bill, I didn't mean to snap. I'm just trying to focus on Will for the moment and then we'll, em ... *[he now addresses the entire class]* Listen, you guys and girls. For the next two weeks we will be living together, eating together, sleeping together and learning together. Begin this two weeks knowing that we are all individuals with individual personalities and individual backgrounds. If we wish to discuss those with each other that's fine. If we don't we must also respect that. There is one thing we all have in common: each one of you want to change your life. Am I right?

[They all begin to nod slowly.]

JOE: What about you, Will. Wouldn't you like to

change your life?

[WILL *looks up at* JOE *like a chastised little boy.*]

WILL: Yes.

JOE: And you, Bill. You too want to change some parts of your life?

BILL: Well, in fairness, nothing that I can think of. But we'll see as the course progresses.

JOE: Ok, Bill, let's see. But I would ask you to do one thing: be as truthful as you possibly can. Now let's move on. Our next principle is Need. Once you establish a need you will think of the solution. Tina, what's your need?

TINA: I need to be a successful businesswoman.

JOE: Good ... And what are you doing about it?

TINA: I came here ... that's the first step.

JOE: Well done, Tina, and the biggest step of all, and the right step, I think. Tina should get a round of applause.

[*Everybody claps.* BEN *raises his hand.*]

JOE: Ben, do you have a need?

BEN: Yes, Mr Daly.

JOE: Good. I'll come to you in a minute. But first, Tony, what's your need?

TONY: I've spent my life working to the clock,

doing what I'm supposed to do, doing what I was told to do. I need to work to *my* clock, I need to do things *my* way, I need to do what *I* want to do.

JOE: And have you begun, Tony?

TONY: Everybody said I was crazy to take this course. My wife didn't even speak to me on Monday morning when I was leaving the house. But I have decided not to let anybody tell me what to do anymore!

JOE: Sit down, Tony. That's the kind of determination that's necessary to succeed, the determination to go on even when everybody around you is telling you what you're doing is crazy.

[BEN *again raises his hand.*]

JOE: Yes, Ben, do you have a need?

BEN: Yes, Mr Daly.

JOE: Well, come on, out with it.

BEN: I need to piss.

[*Everybody laughs including* JOE.]

JOE: Well, go ahead then, Ben, that's a need that must be fulfilled immediately ... with enthusiasm.

[BEN *scurries out of the room.* JOE *returns to the flip chart and turns a new page and writes Carolina Nod on the page. He turns back to face the class.*]

JOE: What's the Carolina Nod? Let me give you a quick example.

> *[JOE walks to TONY and proffers his hand as if for a handshake. TONY takes his hand and JOE begins to nod his head, so does TONY.]*

JOE: Manchester United won the First Division title in 1974, isn't that true?

TONY: Yes.

> *[JOE turns to the class.]*

JOE: Manchester United did not win the title in 1974 and Tony probably didn't know if they did or not, am I right, Tony?

TONY: I haven't a clue about football.

JOE: Then why did you agree with me? Why did you say yes?

TONY: I ... I don't know.

JOE: Because I used the Carolina Nod. When you are eye to eye with someone and you nod your head and ask a positive question the reply will be positive because it's impossible to say no while you're nodding your head. It's that simple.

WILL: It can't be that simple on everyone.

JOE: Amazing as it sounds, yes, it is.

BILL: Personally, Mr Daly, I think we were all kind

of expecting that, and that's why Tony agreed with you. What if you tried it on somebody who wasn't expecting it?

[*BEN re-enters the room.*]

JOE: Well, let's see, shall we? Ben, come around here.

[*BEN walks to the front of the class.*]

BEN: What?

[*JOE extends his hand, BEN takes it. Staring at BEN, JOE slowly pulls his back and starts wiping it with his pocket handkerchief. He hands it to BEN.*]

JOE: Here, dry your hand.

[*BEN dries his hand and JOE begins the process again, extending his hand and taking BEN's. JOE begins to nod, BEN begins to nod back.*]

JOE: Ben, Manchester United were First Division Champions in 1974, isn't that true?

BEN: [*still nodding*] No, Derby County were.

[*The class erupts into laughter.*]

BEN: They were. Jesus, did I miss a football quiz?

JOE: Go back to your seat, Ben. Look, people, trust me. I have used the Carolina Nod in the field: it works *[he glances at* BEN] on normal people.

[JOE walks to the files and passes a file to each person. JOE extracts an insurance policy from his file.]

JOE: Open your file and you will see one of these on the top of your papers.

[They all extract their insurance policy.]

JOE: Hold it up in the air, like this, up in the air. This is the key to your fortune. What you're looking at is a Personal Accident Policy.

[As JOE says this he writes "PAP" on the flip chart.]

JOE: Personal ... Accident ... Policy. In the business we call this a PAP, wanna know why?

WILL: Because it's only for suckers.

[Everybody laughs. JOE goes on, completely ignoring WILL's comment.]

JOE: The reason we call them PAP is because this is the DADDY of all policies. Statistics have shown that it is virtually impossible for any of us to go through our life, without at some stage having an accident. When this happens to one of your clients they will bless the day that *you* walked through their door. For you will have guaranteed your client two hundred and fifty pounds a week every week for as long as he remains hospitalised as the result of a personal accident not associated with work, sport, airplanes, boats or transport of any kind. And all it's going to cost him is thirty pounds a year. Isn't that fantastic?

BILL: Absolutely ... Although I would like to hear more about the not connected with work, sport, trains, boats, planes or any form of transport, part!

JOE: Those are technicalities and we'll come to those much later in the course. First, we have to establish a *belief* in the product.

   [*JOE holds the policy in the air for all to see.*]

JOE: This is the product. Anyone who does not believe *this* is value for money get up and leave this course now. I mean it: get up and leave the room.

   [*JOE glances around again for reaction. Nobody moves.*]

JOE: Good. Now! [*he walks towards BEN*] I hear you ask–

BEN: I never opened me mouth. Why are ye picking on me?

JOE: That's merely a figure of speech, Ben, but I'm still sure you would like to know what's in it for you. How much money can Ben expect to make?

BEN: A thousand pounds a week.

JOE: What?

BEN: A thousand pounds a week. That's what it said in the ad in the paper.

[Everybody chirps in with mutters of agreement: that's what they also saw in the ad in the paper.]

JOE: Indeed, that is possible, and more.

[JOE walks behind pupils and pulls on a cord that pulls down a huge photograph of a good-looking man. JOE points to the picture. His face is full of admiration.]

JOE: He makes more than that. Last year *he* made over one hundred thousand pounds.

[JOE again glances around nodding his head. They all look in awe at the photograph.]

JOE: This is Bob Voice, the company's top salesman in Europe. And do you know where Bob Voice was just a little over twelve months ago?

[JOE walks around to the front of the pupils. They are shaking their heads.]

JOE: I'll tell you: right there.

[JOE points dramatically to where TONY is sit-

ting. Everybody gasps in awe. JOE *becomes a little self-congratulatory.]*

JOE: Yes, indeed, my star pupil is good old Bob. His first week in the field he broke the First Week in the Field Record Sales. His first month in the field he broke the European First Month in the Field Record. By the time he'd been in the field six months he had broken all the records, even the American ones. Yet no more than a year and a half ago, he sat in that chair, just like Tony. Sure he was a loser, just like Tony; oh, he'd been in and out of dead-end jobs. But the day he sat in that chair for the first time ... changed his life.

[JOE walks around and slowly pushes the picture back up. Smugly he turns to the class.]

JOE: I'm pretty proud of Bob Voice. I did a good job, even though I do say so myself.

[EMILY starts a little applause and they all join in.]

JOE: Steady, steady now, come on. I want you to save your applause for your graduation day here, then you can clap. Then you can look at me and say "Thank you, Joe. Thank you for showing me my options, Joe."

TINA: Options? Yeh seen one fella's options, yeh seen them all.

[EMILY *stares at* TINA.]

FADE OUT

Scene Three

[*A pub. Two lounge tables, with ashtrays and glasses. Around the tables are six chairs. Slide 4 reads: "Residents' Lounge, That Evening." The only one seated in the lounge is* WILL. *Enter* TINA.]

TINA: Joe Daly's not in here Will, is he?

WILL: 'Course he is. Can't yeh see him there tap dancin' in the fuckin' ashtray?

TINA: Don't be smart. I just mean since we're

47

supposed to be up studying, I didn't want to come in for a drink here if he's gonna be here as well.

[TINA goes side stage and calls.]

TINA: Emily ... Emily, come on. The coast is clear.

[EMILY enters and they both sit down.]

TINA: Where's Bill gone?

EMILY: To the bar to get us a drink.

TINA: Ah, fair play to him.

[Enter TONY and BEN.]

WILL: Over here, lads. I have a pint for yis.

[The two boys join WILL.]

TONY: Thanks a lot, Will.

BEN: Fair play to yeh, Will. Jesus, this is great. I haven't mitched from class since I was fifteen.

TONY: *[to WILL]* I've never mitched.

WILL: Do I look fuckin' surprised?

[There's a few moments silence.]

TINA: This course is a lot tougher than I thought it would be. I really can't see myself making it to the end.

WILL: Would yeh give a fuck?

TINA: Well, actually, yes, I would. This course is important to me and I want to pass.

WILL: Huh. *[he shrugs]*

BEN: Jesus, I have to pass it, otherwise me father will make me take over the farm.

TONY: Oh, you have a farm then, Ben?

BEN: Well, me father has and he's great ideas that I might take it over, but, Jesus, it's not for me.

TONY: Gosh, I thought it was every young farmer's son's dream to some day own the family farm.

WILL: Young man's dream, ha! Tony, dreams are only for children.

BEN: Well, it's not my dream I'll tell yeh that, oh God no. Sure it would break your heart.

EMILY: I know what you mean, Ben, I had a cat once.

TINA: I don't think that's what he means, Emily. I think he's talkin' about it bein' hard work, isn't that right, Ben?

BEN: Yeh, that's it, Tina. Three hundred and sixty-five days a year that herd has to be milked. That's forty-two thousand tits to be pulled per annum then off to the disco Friday night to get blotto, dig yer hand into your pocket to come up with the price of a pint and your pockets full of tractor parts and, ah ... Jesus, no, not for me.

[BILL enters the lounge. He is carrying three drinks.]

BILL: Here we are, girls. A pale sherry for you, Emily dear, and a pint of cider for you I believe, Tina.

TINA: Thanks, Bill. Ben was just telling us about his father's farm.

BILL: Oh, indeed. My own father had a farm of sorts. A thousand acres you know.

WILL: Where? Where was the farm?

BILL: Em, in the country.

WILL: What part of the country?

BILL: Em, midlands, well, south, em, kind of south midlands.

WILL: You're a fuckin' liar! I wouldn't believe the "Our Father" out of your mouth.

BILL: No, it's true, in fact we actually have the best prize bulls in the country. Daddy won many an award at the, em, Spring Show.

BEN: My dad bought a prize bull. Jesus, that was a hell of a story.

EMILY: Why, what happened?

BEN: He paid five thousand pounds for it.

BILL: Five thousand pound? That's a lot of bull.

BEN: So is your fuckin' story.

TONY: What happened, Ben, what happened to the bull?

BEN: Me dad brought him home, tied him up outside the kitchen door. We were just having our tea and the next thing we heard a big bang outside the door of the kitchen. Me father and me got up and opened the kitchen door: there was the whore of a bull lying stone dead, and me da only after buying him six hours before.

BILL: Good grief! So what did your father do?

BEN: *[takes a mouthful of his pint]* He kicked the bollix out of him.

[They all sit in stunned silence. BEN takes another mouthful.]

BEN: Ah, farming. Sure it would break your heart.

TINA: I nearly married a farmer once.

TONY: Did you, Tina?

TINA: Yeh, fifty-five he was. Said he loved me, said I made him feel younger.

WILL: I can imagine. He must've had a few bob, did he?

TINA: I don't know, actually, I liked him a lot, an awful lot.

EMILY: But yeh didn't love him Tina, no? Is that why you didn't marry him?

TINA: No, it wasn't that. He called it off! He said his ma wouldn't let him.

BEN: That'd be typical of a farmer's mother! My ma had the wife all picked out for me: Heather Flannigan. She won the Ballincoyle Maiden title in 1993.

TONY: That sounds like a horse race. Oh sorry, Ben, I didn't mean any disrespect!

BEN: Oh, yer all right, Tony, you're not far wrong! It's a race over one hundred yards carrying a young bullock across your shoulders.

EMILY: Not a beauty contest then?

TONY: Not a bit of it. Beauty? Jesus, nobody ever called Heather a beauty. She was built like a bouncer and had a face on her like a cow licking piss off a nettle.

   [All laugh.]

WILL: Fair play to yeh, Ben. Yeh have a good sense of humour.

BEN: It hasn't all been doom and gloom. I met a beautiful redhead on foreign holidays once. She came home with me. We lived together for six months.

EMILY: It didn't work out then?

BEN: Ah, I don't think she was really into me, she was already married and she wasn't happy. I think I was just a reason for her to get away.

EMILY: What about you two, Will and Tony, are you two married?

TONY: I am. To Linda. Twenty years.

TINA: And?

TONY: And that's it. I met her when I was fifteen, she was my first girlfriend. Six years later her and her mother decided it was time we got married. So we did. That's that!

BILL: No exciting romantic stories to regale us with, Tony ?

TONY: What? No. Linda's not that type, yeh know, she's not the dreamy romantic kind. She's more, eh, fuckin' boring actually.

[All laugh.]

BILL: Well, I have had my share of romances. I've made love in every possible position: lying down, standing up, in a jet airplane, naked under a full moon in Hawaii. On one occasion I even had a woman with me!

[All laugh.]

EMILY: What about you, Will? Are you married?

WILL: I was ... once. Red-haired bitch! I gave her everything but all she could do was nag, nag, nag. "Where were you till this hour? You're always drunk. Yeh never come home." There was no fuckin' pleasin' her.

TINA: Jaysus, I wonder why.

EMILY: So you two are ... separated?

WILL: Not officially. She just fucked off. She went on holidays to Turkey with her sister, met some bloke, never seen her since.

[All look at BEN.]

BEN: I've never been to Turkey in me fuckin' life.

[WILL rises and, standing, empties his glass.]

WILL: I'm off to the bar for another drink. Anyone want one?

BEN: Em, no thanks, Will, I'm goin' on up to study.

WILL: Study me arse. None of the PMA crap will be of any use to you at all, Tony, am I right?

[TONY hangs his head sheepishly.]

TONY: Well, I don't know, Will. I'm going up to study as well. I'm going to give this thing a few days. It's tough but I want to give it a try.

TINA: 'Course yeh do, Tony, we all do, that's why we're here. We wouldn't have started it unless we intended to finish it.

WILL: Finish it, me arse. As soon as I have me first week out of the way ye won't see me back here.

[WILL *leaves*. BEN *stands and empties his glass.*]

BEN: I'm off to study. Goodnight.

TONY: Hang on, Ben, I'll go up with you.

[BEN *and* TONY *leave together.* BILL *stands.*]

BILL: Ladies, another drink?

EMILY: Well, not really. One is my limit, so Bernard says.

TINA: I'm grand, Bill, anyway it's my round.

BILL: Nonsense! If you girls aren't going to join me I think I'll leave it at just the one. Right then, I'm off to bed to study my lines.

[BILL *leaves.*]

EMILY: He's a real gentleman Bill, isn't he?

TINA: Ah, he's very nice, although I do think he's a bit of a spoofer. That Will fellow is a real bastard, isn't he?

EMILY: Well, I don't know. He's a bit grumpy all right, but I think there's more to our Will than meets the eye – he seems like a lonely old soul.

TINA: Would you blame his wife. Imagine havin' to ...[*pause*] Lonely? Well, I know how that feels.

EMILY: No boyfriend then?

TINA: Nah, it's hard to get a fella in my line of work.

EMILY: Too busy?

[*TINA stares at EMILY for a moment.*]

TINA: Yeh, too busy. Mind you there's a fella has the apartment underneath mine and he's been askin' me out every Saturday night without fail for the last six months, but I've always been workin'.

EMILY: Well, you're not workin' this Saturday are you?

TINA: No, I'm not.

EMILY: What's his name, this chap in the apartment below you?

TINA: Roger. He's a fireman: a big, huge hunk of a man with a huge hose as well. [*She laughs.*]

EMILY: Bernard has a big nose.

TINA: Hose! A huge hose. Yeh know, a big mickey. [*She gestures.*]

EMILY: Ooh! Bernard hasn't got one of those. I mean not huge, just average. But you know they're all the same size when they're erect!

TINA: Who told you that? Let me guess ... Bernard? [*pauses*] The girls I share with call him Roger Ramjet.

EMILY: Roger Ramjet, is he a politician?

TINA: Roger Ramjet off the telly.

EMILY: Oh, I'm sorry, I'm afraid the only one off the telly I know is Gay Byrne. I don't know any of these new comedians.

TINA: He's not a comedian, he's a super ... ah, it doesn't matter.

EMILY: Well, my advice to you, Tina, is, if Mr Ramjet asks you out this Saturday say yes. Go on, you deserve it.

TINA: You're right Emily, I do. I think I will.

[WILL *enters and sits down just as the two women are getting ready to leave.*]

TINA: You not goin' up to study then, Will?

WILL: Study me arse.

TINA: [*over her shoulder*] I did, and you've a huge one.

[WILL *snaps a look over his shoulder: the women are gone.*]

Scene Four

[The meeting room. Slide 5 reads: "Half-time Result – Class 6: Joe Daly 0." JOE is at the flip chart. The legend "PMA" is on the chart. He taps the chart and speaks.]

JOE: So what we've learned all this week is that big sales are not possible without a positive mental attitude. I mean, ask yourself what's the first thing you usually do every morning? *[walks around the table]* Emily?

EMILY: Well, a lot depends on what Bernard is doing. If he is working I would usually prepare his breakfast and polish his shoes and have them ready for him. Bernard likes his shoes gleaming. Or if it's a Saturday I'd bring his clubs in from the garage and leave them ready, always remembering to clean out the grooves in his nine iron and pitching wedge. If it's Sunday I usually go to

Mass, well not so much to Mass as down to the church to get Bernard's papers for him, he likes a paper with his breakfast on a Sunday morning.

TINA: Jaysus! Does Bernard get you to wipe his arse for him?

EMILY: Well, only if his arthritis–

JOE: Enough! Tina, what's the first thing you do every morning?

TINA: I usually collect me knickers and do me lodgement on the way home.

JOE: *[flustered]* Will ... the first thing you do?

WILL: I'll have a smoke and a glass of brandy to get me heart started.

JOE: Tony?

TONY: Well, I-I-I–

JOE: I'll get back to you, Tony. Bill!

BILL: Ah, I do my exercises: down one two, up one two and then the other shoelace. Ha, ha, ha, ha, only kidding. Actually I don't have a set routine, I can't recall what I do in the mornings. In fact, I can't recall what I did this morning.

JOE: I'll accept that!

BILL: How kind of you.

JOE: And Ben?

BEN: Have a shite usually.

BILL: Oh, I thought you meant after that, Joe.

JOE: Right, for the next two weeks this is what you are going to do. You're going to get up, you're going to walk to the mirror in your room, you're going to look in that mirror and see the person looking at you in the reflection ... and you're going to say "I feel fantastic." Come on, let's try it everybody.

> [JOE *leads them. There's a general mumble of "I feel fantastic". JOE stops them and starts again. The mumble gets louder. He stops and starts them until it's a screech "I feel fantastic". By this stage the group are waving their hands in the air, smiling and playing along.*]

JOE: [*enthusiastically*] Great. Well, if I meet you on the corridor, or I meet you downstairs in the lobby, or I meet you here in the room and I say to you "How's your PMA today?" you reply "fantastic".

JOE: Emily, how's your PMA?

EMILY: Fantastic!

JOE: Tina, how's your PMA?

TINA: Fantastic!

JOE: Tony, how's your PMA?

TONY: F-F-Faaa–

JOE: I'll get back to you, Tony. Ben, how's your PMA?

BEN: Fuckin' great, boy.

JOE: Ben, if I ask you "How's your PMA today?" you simply say "fantastic!" Can we do that ?

BEN: Let's do it again.

JOE: Ben, how's your PMA today?

BEN: Fantastic ... boy!

JOE: I suppose that'll do.

> [JOE *turns towards the flip chart.* BURT *stands up and walks to the side of the room.*]

BURT: Can I see you for a moment, Mr Daly, please?

> [JOE *looking a little perplexed, turns on his heel and the two men move front of stage.*]

JOE: What's this about now?

BURT: I notice when that Ben chap said "fantastic boy", you said that's close enough. This is a problem with you, Mr Daly: "close enough" will not do. It must be word for word. This is the only way to teach the system: word for word.

JOE: I'm quite aware of how the system must be taught. I have been teaching it for eight years. But at this stage in the course it is not necessary for the PMA section to be taught word for word.

BURT: In the training manual it says it is.

JOE: That's ridiculous. It's not in the training manual.

BURT: *[extracting manual]* Well, let's step outside and have a look at the manual, shall we?

JOE: *[to class]* Myself and Mr Rubenstein are about to confer on something, it should not take more than a couple of minutes. In the meantime why don't you all amuse yourselves?

> *[JOE and BURT leave the room. Meantime back in the room ...]*

TINA: Amuse ourselves. I mean how are we supposed to amuse ourselves?

WILL: I'll give you a few ideas, honey.

TINA: Yeh, well you'd want to get yourself a pocketful of money and plastic surgery.

> *[EMILY giggles.]*

TONY: In the garage I used to write down the registration letters of all the buses and try and make as many words as I could out of them. That's how I'd amuse myself.

WILL: Tony, are you on fuckin' drugs?

BILL: Wait a minute, I have one. What about this: I'm looking at a picture on the wall and I make the following statement "That man's father is my father's son". Now, who is in the picture?

WILL: I heard that one before. It's yourself.

BILL: Quite correct, yes, it is rather an old one.

BEN: I have one. *[BEN stands, goes to the flip chart and turns over to the next page. He writes the numbers 12, 14, 16, 21 and 24. He turns to the group, who are studying the numbers.]* Which is the odd one out?

[The group studies the flip chart.]

WILL: You're the fuckin' odd one out. Stand out of the way, will yeh?

[Some are writing the figures down, Tony in particular.]

TONY: Well, there is no logical secret sequence to the numbers and although some of them can be divided by a single number, not all of them can. I'm afraid you have me.

BILL: Yes, Ben, you have me too.

[A look of excitement comes over BEN's face, delighted that he has fooled everybody.]

TINA: I give up.

EMILY: I haven't a clue.

BEN: It's a good one, isn't it?

TONY: Well, don't keep us in suspense: which *is* the odd one out?

BEN: Twenty-four.

EMILY: And, em, why is twenty-four the odd one out?

BEN: Well, all these ones are served with rice, twenty-four comes on its own.

WILL: What the fuck is he talkin' about?

BILL: Eh, nice one, Ben, but I think it's a bit of a parochial one. One would have to know the menu in your local Chinese.

BEN: I have some copies of it with me. Would you like to see it?

BILL: Not right now.

BEN: Will I do another one?

WILL: Sit down, yeh gobshite.

[BURT *and* JOE *re-enter.*]

JOE: Well, I've never seen that before.

BURT: Well, you see it now.

JOE: Right. Mr Rubenstein, can I ask you, unless it is an absolute emergency, please don't call me outside the door again.

BURT: On the contrary, Mr Daly, if at any stage I see you deviating from the system I shall indeed bring you outside, or would you prefer I discuss it in front of the pupils?

JOE: *[doesn't answer but indignantly crosses the room announcing]* All right everybody, you have all done very well this week but I still feel a little revision is in order. So take out your training manual and go to page one where we will find our opening sales statement. I'm sure you have all learned this off by heart by now, but still let's begin with a reading.

[Everybody extracts their manual.]

JOE: All right! "Good morning, Mr O'Brien. I've just been in with Mr Connolly next door and I believe I have something here which will interest you." Now why do we say this? We say this because we want to gain Mr O'Brien's attention as well as add a little intrigue. His obvious reply is: "Why what is it?", which gives us the opportunity to say "I'm glad you asked. Let me come in and show you", at which point we are in the door. Good, isn't it? Right, now let's try it without the book, and this time I want you to do it with a smile and a handshake. So let's try all that together.

[The class, in unison, begins to say the opening pitch.]

JOE: Good ... Emily.

EMILY: Good morning Mr O'Brien. I've just been in with Mr Connolly next door and I believe I have something here which will interest you.

JOE: Well done, Emily.

[They all clap.]

JOE: Tony!

TONY: Go-go—

JOE: I'll get back to you, Tony.

JOE: Now, Bill!

Bill: *[stands]* Good morning, Mr O'Brien. I've just been in with Mr Connolly next door and I believe I have something here that will interest you.

JOE: Well done, Bill. Bill gets a round of applause for that, come on.

[Everybody claps.]

JOE: Excellent, a good start. I think we are going to do well.

[He looks over at BURT who looks matter-of-fact, crosses his legs and crosses his arms. BEN puts his hand up.]

JOE: Yes, Ben?

BEN: What if his name is not Mr O'Brien?

JOE: This is just an example, Ben. Of course his name won't be Mr O'Brien.

[BEN still with the hand up.]

JOE: Now what, Ben?

BEN: Well, it could be Mr O'Brien. There's a few

Mr O'Briens in an estate near us, but now I'm not sure if any of them live next door to a Connolly.

JOE: Ben, we find two houses beside each other and we use the names of the two people inside the houses.

BEN: Well, how do we know the name?

JOE: *[now frustrated]* I'll come to that fucking later!

[BURT is not impressed. JOE walks tentatively towards him.]

JOE: That's a little Gaelic.

[BILL raises his hand.]

JOE: Yes, Bill?

BILL: Em, does Ben get a round of applause for that?

JOE: *[staring]* No.

[JOE now walks back to the flip chart, turns to a new page and writes the word "RENEWALS" on the board. He puts his marker down and turns to the class.]

JOE: Now, those are the opening lines when selling a new policy. However, you in the field will also be renewing old policies. These are called renewals.

BILL: Hm ... an interesting name.

JOE: You must try and remember always, in the field, that you are sales persons and the object of the exercise is to sell. Instead of just renewing the old PAP Policy we now try and move the client up to a Full Longterm Overall Policy.

BILL: Or FLOP.

JOE: Thank you, Bill. We prefer to call it FLO ... FLO. This is an excellent policy and only offered to those people who have been with the company for more than one year. This offers full accident coverage in any country in the world, provided the accident is not to do with planes, trains, boats, automobiles or sporting activity, work or while on holiday.

WILL: Sure, why would a person be in another country if he wasn't on holiday or working?

JOE: You'd be surprised, Will.

WILL: I'd be fuckin' amazed.

JOE: Will, I want you to concentrate on not injecting any negatives into our programme.

[JOE *turns to the class.*]

JOE: From time to time we all face challenges in our lives and these challenges sometimes lead us to become negative in what we are approaching. Will has one or two personal challenges which he must overcome. But believe me, Will, negativity is not the route to take. You must be positive, Will.

WILL: I am positive.

JOE: Good.

WILL: I'm positive that this is a load of shite.

JOE: Will, put your hand in your pocket and give me twenty pounds.

WILL: I will in me arse.

JOE: Please, just for a moment.

[WILL *draws out twenty pounds and hands it to* JOE.]

JOE: Thank you, Will. Now, Will, I'm going to leave that twenty pounds over here on this table right here under this glass. That's your twenty pounds, Will. Now, Will, you're cycling home from a friend's house at dusk, minding your own business, listening to the last of the birds tweet their way to sleep. Suddenly around the corner comes a speeding car. *Crash!* The bike goes twenty yards down the road and you go ten yards in the air. *Splat!* You land on the ground, Will. *Be Baw, Be Baw!* The ambulance comes along and takes you away. Because of this accident, Will, you are in hospital for three weeks, ok?

WILL: Ok!

[JOE *walks to the table and takes the twenty*

pounds, goes over and slaps it on the table in front of WILL.]

JOE: Now, Will. See how far that twenty pounds will get you in those three weeks.

[WILL picks up the twenty pounds and stares at it. He looks at the others in the class: they all look at him disgustedly. WILL starts to look a little sad.]

JOE: On the other hand, Will, if you give me that twenty pounds for a PAP I'll give you two hundred and fifty pounds for every week you are in that hospital.

BEN: Fair fuckin' play to yeh, you're a decent man.

[All of the class clap. Disgruntled, WILL puts his twenty pounds into his pocket. JOE triumphantly walks back to the flip chart.]

JOE: Now, let's get back to work.

[JOE suddenly looks at his watch.]

JOE: Well, dearie me, it seems we've run out of time. That's been a good first week, but still over the weekend I want you all to study the points that we've been through and we'll have a short test on Monday.

[Everybody rises and heads for the door.]

JOE: Stop! Not yet. We must finish with our posi session. Everybody hold your file and your clipboard under your arm.

[They all do what's asked.]

JOE: I want you to step back from your seat and start marching on the spot in unison.

[After a bit of a shambles they get into step. JOE walks to the front of the line and begins to lead the way.]

JOE: Now, everybody out loud: "Hi ho, hi ho, it's off to work we go, with our file and clip and our PMA, hi ho, hi ho," all together.

[They all begin to sing. JOE marches them around the table a couple of times and then he holds the door open as they all exit. Then he closes the door behind them. JOE walks to his desk to begin tidying up his things. BURT stands and approaches him.]

BURT: I thought you handled that very well.

JOE: Why thank you, Burt. It's all just part of being a tutor.

BURT: One victory does not win the war.

JOE: Well, I wasn't aware we were at war.

BURT: Well, we are. You see, I've checked all of

your candidates in the field and the only word that comes to mind is disgraceful.

[JOE walks to the back wall and pulls down the roller chart to reveal his star pupil's photograph.]

JOE: Disgraceful, yes? What about this? What about the top salesman in the field? He came out of this class.

BURT: Probably.

JOE: He broke all the records.

BURT: That's correct.

JOE: He took in more money than any rep in Europe.

BURT: That's also correct.

JOE: So don't talk to me about disgraceful.

BURT: You're right. He was the top salesman in the field and he did break all the records and he did in fact take in the most money in Europe. The problem is he didn't hand any of it over to the company.

[JOE stares at BURT dumbfounded. There is silence for a moment. JOE quickly pulls the cord that sends the photograph back up into the roll.]

JOE: I knew he was a slimy bastard the minute he walked in this door. I said so in my report to head office.

BURT: No, you didn't, Joe. Not only did you not say that, you put him out in the field. He's your star pupil, Joe! I'll see you Monday – have a great weekend!

> [BURT *exits. JOE turns to the wall and slowly pulls the photograph down again. He walks, shoulders drooping, to the door and opens it. He turns to the photograph and shouts*] Bastard! [*He leaves the room.*]

END OF FIRST HALF

ACT TWO

Scene One

[Slide 6: "End of Week Two, Day One." Lights come up to show the classroom with JOE *in the middle of a sales talk.]*

JOE: I don't know how many times I've seen this happen. Oh, I see the sales people do all the hard work but they can't make the close. Once you have presented the sales pitch go straight to the close by saying, "Now, if you don't mind, I'd like to begin writing this for you, and your first name is?"

BEN: Ben.

[JOE stares at BEN hopelessly.]

JOE: *[moving on]* That's where your rebuttals come in and by now I'm sure you have them all off.

[JOE sees WILL is asleep. JOE kicks him under

the table and WILL *comes awakes with a start.]*

WILL: Sorry, Joe, I just dozed off.

JOE: Welcome back, Will. Indeed, welcome back all of you. *[looks at his watch]* Okay, that's it everybody. Finish your notes and we'll take a break for lunch I'll see you back here at two o'clock. Well done, nice to see you all back. *[turns to* BURT] Please excuse me for a few minutes, Mr Rubenstein.

[JOE exits. The class begin to disperse.]

EMILY: So, Tina, how did things go on Saturday night with Roger Ramjet?

TINA: Oh Emily, don't talk to me. Here was me hopin' for a hose and he arrived with a whole bleedin' fire engine.

[The two laugh.]

TINA: How's Bernard?

EMILY: Bernard ... oh, well, I hardly saw him. He was away all day Saturday and returned home on Sunday morning just in time to pick up his clubs. He had a competition. He's fine ... I'm sure.

TINA: Ah, never mind Bernard. Come on, let's go. I've loads to tell you.

[They leave.]

BILL: I didn't expect to see you back this week.

WILL: You're not seein' me. It's your fuckin' imagination, like all the other things yeh see.

BEN: But I see it too.

WILL: No, yeh don't really, that's just him convincin' yeh that yeh see me, and you believe him 'cause you're a fool.

BEN: I know.

TONY: No, you're not a fool, Ben, don't mind him. Will is just messing, aren't you, Will?

WILL: Jaysus, Tony, yeh want to mind you don't fall off that fence. One of these days yeh will and you'll break your fuckin' neck.

[Exit WILL.]

BILL: Oh, I see Wurzel Gummidge has his happy head on today.

[They leave as JOE returns carrying a newspaper. He closes the door. BURT rises from his chair and walks to the pupils' tables, turns some of their notes around and reads them.]

BURT: Pitiful.

JOE: What's that, Burt?

BURT: I said pitiful, Joe, that's what I said, I said pitiful.

79

JOE: What's pitiful?

[BURT *picks up somebody's notes and tosses them back on the table.*]

BURT: This is, they are, you are. The whole God-damn mess is.

JOE: I think they're doing okay.

BURT: Yes, you probably do, Joe. They're all going to fail and you're going to tell me they did their best.

JOE: Well, I believe they are doing their best. They are a little limited.

BURT: A little limited? Those guys are losers.

[JOE *walks away from* BURT. TONY *half-enters the door of the room.*]

BURT: And you're going to lose your job. I meant what I said, Joe: if seventy percent of this class doesn't pass you're out of a job. There will be no appealing, no second chances.

[JOE *turns and sees* TONY *half in and half out of the door.*]

JOE: Eh, Tony, can I help you?

TONY: Eh, no, I just left my notes behind.

[TONY *goes to the table, quickly collects his notes, leaves and closes the door.* BURT *looks after him*

JOE: "Hello, Major Accident Sales Course, Joe Daly speaking, can I help you?"

Week One, Day One "the Magnificent Six".

JOE: "What about you, Will. Wouldn't you like to change your life?"

BEN: " ... it would break your heart ... forty-two thousand tits to be pulled per annum, then off to the disco Friday night to get blotto and your pockets full of tractor parts and ah Jesus no, not for me."

BILL: "Well, I have had my share of romances."

TINA: "So do you, Emily ... except you get paid by the week ...
I get it by the ride."

BEN: "What if his name is not Mr O'Brien?"

WILL: "Wait a minute ... we're not losers ... remember the principles of PMA."

EMILY: "You ... you do the bonky bonky thing ... for money!"

TINA: "There's this fella ... Roger ... he's a fireman, a big huge hunk of a man, with a huge hose as well."

Will "the knife" Benson.

ALL: "Now they are doers, now they are winners, they have a part to play, never in doubt as to what they can do ... with their PMA!"

and then turns back to JOE.]

BURT: Huh! I should have known that was his shit.

JOE: Let me tell you something, Burt. They are doing their best and I believe they will pass.

BURT: They haven't got a hope.

JOE: They probably won't have a hope with you marking the exam papers.

BURT: And what's that supposed to mean?

JOE: You're clever, Burt, you can work that out.

BURT: Are you saying you think I might cheat you, Joe?

JOE: No, not cheat me, cheat them. It's been obvious since you came into this class, Burt, you want me off the company's payroll. Well, if that's the case just fire me, it's not necessary to go through this charade. Regardless of how well any of those pupils do, if you want me out, Burt, all you've got to do is mark them *fail*. I'm not saying that's what you have in mind but don't tell me it's not a possibility.

BURT: Joe, I will tell you it's not a possibility. I've worked for Major Accident for over fifteen years. I started in the field, I spent a year giving this course and now I'm the company controller. During that time I've been called ruthless, I've been called ambitious and I've been called one hungry bastard!

JOE: *[aside]* No, I couldn't believe that!

BURT: But one thing I've always been known for and that is that I'm fair: my integrity has never been in question. Joe, I swear to you anyone who passes that exam I will mark pass, and anyone who fails I will mark fail. Don't expect any favours but I'm telling you now, you won't be cheated.

JOE: Good. I accept that.

[BURT *walks to the door.*]

BURT: It doesn't really matter, Joe, 'cause these guys are heading for the failure list.

JOE: You're wrong. They're doing their best and they will pass!

BURT: You really believe that?

JOE: With all my heart and soul.

BURT: Ha!

[*Exit* BURT. JOE *leafs through the newspaper, picks up the phone, dials a number and speaks.*]

JOE: Hello, I'm calling about the job you advertised in the paper on Friday ...

End of scene.

FADE OUT

Scene Two

[EMILY *and* TINA *are each sitting on a bed. They are going over the study papers. Slide 7 reads: "The Worms Turn." EMILY is slightly drunk.*]

TINA: I don't understand these rebuttals.

EMILY: Why not? Which one do you mean?

TINA: All of them, the whole principle of the thing: always agree with the customer. How can you always agree with the customer if he's telling you he doesn't want something and you're still trying to sell it to him? It just doesn't make sense.

[EMILY *stands.*]

EMILY: Of course it does, Tina, just agree with the customer. For instance if he says "I don't want it", you immediately say "Tell me, do you have a car?" He answers "Yes". You say "Good, because most people who drive cars find that this is exactly the extra policy they need. Let me show you ..." And on you go with your sales pitch.

TINA: What if he says "No, I don't have a car. I have a bike?"

EMILY: You immediately say "That's the very reason you need it. Let's face it, Mr X, if you're cycling along on your bicycle, not breaking any law and just taking your time on your way home, some lunatic comes around the corner in a car ... When the two meet in a crash who do you think is going to come off the worst? It'll be you, won't it, Mr X?" Use the Carolina Nod and he will say "Yes". Then you go "So let me show you why this will help ease your mind".

TINA: Okay, right. What if he says "No, I don't have a car at all, or a bike."

EMILY: Come on, Tina, it works! The company has been using it for fifty years. They know it works and I believe it does.

[They go back to their study papers. EMILY closes her book, gets up and pours a whiskey. She turns and sighs. TINA looks up.]

TINA: What?

EMILY: Oh nothing, nothing ... nothing to do with the course. I was just thinking about Bernard.

You know, he's hoping I'll come back from this course with some of my problems sorted out.

TINA: Emily, if you don't mind me sayin' so – ah, nothing.

EMILY: No, please, Tina, go on, what?

TINA: I think Bernard is your problem.

EMILY: Oh no, Tina. Bernard's a wonderful man!

TINA: He's a prick, Emily. Sure he's been on the phone twenty times in the last week. "Where's me socks? Where's me golf clubs? How do you work the cooker?"

EMILY: Oh Tina, you'll learn when you get married: all men are helpless.

TINA: Not the ones I've met. They're just lazy.

EMILY: Do you know many men, Tina?

[TINA *looks at* EMILY *long and hard and then answers.*]

TINA: Hundreds.

EMILY: So it would be mostly men you would be doing the personal entertaining for?

[TINA *now sits up and closes her own book.*]

TINA: Ah Emily, are you serious?

EMILY: Serious about what?

TINA: Emily, I'm a prostitute. Sorry, I *was* a prostitute!

85

[EMILY stares. There is no response.]

TINA: Are yeh shocked?

EMILY: Yes. I am quite.

TINA: What do yeh find so shocking?

EMILY: You ... you do the bonky bonky thing for money?

TINA: So do you, Emily, except you get paid by the week. I get it by the ride.

[EMILY is aghast. She jumps up and walks to the cabinet, and pours herself a large whiskey and downs it in one gulp, then pours another one. She turns to TINA.]

EMILY: So that's why you wear those ... *[pointing at the bathroom door]* those thingies.

TINA: What thingies?

EMILY: The black fishnet stockings with the suspenders and the red knickers and bra.

TINA: *[laughs]* No Emily, I wear them because I like them. When I put them on I feel really sexy and I like feelin' sexy.

[EMILY downs the whiskey and pours out another. She walks to her bed and slowly sits on the edge. She speaks as if to no one.]

EMILY: I haven't felt sexy in years. I'm not sure if I

ever even did.

TINA: 'Course you're sexy. Mind you, you could do with one or two improvements.

EMILY: Like what?

TINA: Well, the way you walk, the way you sit, the way you look at people, your make-up and your hair.

EMILY: Jesus Christ, that's everything! *[she knocks back the whiskey]* Bernard was right: I'm a dud!

TINA: You're not a fuckin' dud, you just need a bit of work. I'll tell you what, Emily, the boys are comin' up here in ten minutes so we can all study here in our bedroom. When they've gone, you and I will do a little bit of work on *Emily* and how to make her sexy.

EMILY: Would you do that for me, Tina?

TINA: Of course, I will. Now listen, you've had a bit too much to drink. Why don't you go in and have a quick shower and be fresh for when the boys get up here?

[EMILY rises unsteadily.]

EMILY: That's what I'll do: shower, study, then sexy ... Sexy Emily – I like the sound of that.

[EMILY puts her glass down on the table and walks to the bathroom door]

87

EMILY: And when I'm sexy I'm going to have sexy underwear just like yours.

TINA: *[laughs]* Sure, I'll go and help you pick them.

> *[EMILY closes the bathroom door. We hear the shower running and EMILY humming in the shower. There's a knock at the other door. TINA opens it and the boys come in. They all sit in various places around the beds. They all look a little dejected except BILL who never looks dejected. WILL is not with them.]*

TINA: What's wrong with you lot?

BILL: Oh, the boys are a little down.

TINA: Havin' a little trouble with the studies, boys?

BEN: A little trouble? I get as far as "Hello, Mr O'Brien. I've just been in with Mr Connolly next door" and I can't think the fuck what the rest of it is.

TONY: I'm having trouble with my rebuttals.

TINA: Me too.

TONY: I understand that we have to agree with the customer but I get it arse-ways, when the customer says "I don't want it, it's only shit", I agree and leave.

TINA: Where's Will?

BILL: Oh, he'll be up in a couple of minutes. He's

just gone to the lobby to make a phone call.

TINA: Gone to the bar to get a drink, more like it!

TONY: What do you mean, Tina?

TINA: Come on, Tony, don't tell me yeh can't see it. He's an alcoholic, for God's sake.

TONY: No! Will, an alcoholic? I don't believe it!

BEN: Well, I'm not one for gossip but he shares my room and, good God, he does about two bottles of whiskey a night, I swear it!

TINA: That's why he's here, so Joe Daly told me.

TONY: He's here to cure his alcoholism?

TINA: No, no. He's here because he got into trouble with drink on him and when it went to court the judge told him if he didn't get a job and show an improvement he'd slap him in prison. So he's just usin' this as an excuse to stay out of prison. He's no intention of passin' the course or workin' for the company.

BILL: It's a pity because he's doing very well in spots. He has a wonderful memory.

BEN: Ah, he's okay during the day but then at night he drinks himself into a stupor and every morning it's like starting all over again. Be Jaysus, if I was to drink the amount of drink he drinks I'd need a bloody good memory too.

[There is a knock at the door.]

89

BILL: Watch it, everybody, that's him now. Let's not discuss it in front of him.

TONY: Tina, perhaps you'd better put that whiskey bottle away.

[TINA *moves swiftly and puts the whiskey bottle into a drawer.* BILL *opens the door.*]

BILL: Will, how are you? Let me guess: you've just been in with Mr Connolly next door and you have something you think might interest me.

[They all laugh except WILL *who walks in rather disgruntled.*]

BILL: [in Bogart voice] Of all the rooms in all the hotels he has to walk into mine.

WILL: Shut up! And that's "gin joints" not rooms.

BILL: Well, I didn't like to say "gin joints" considering your prob– [he leaves the word "problem" unfinished]

WILL: Considering what? Come on, Bill, considering what?

BILL: [in Ron Moody voice] I'll have you, Bill Sykes. [barks like a dog] Stop it, Bullseye! Bullseye!

WILL: Come on, spit it out! Look at yis, just look at yis.

[He walks over to BEN.]

WILL: Having a little natter were we, Ben? Oh "Will likes his drink" *[he mimics Ben]* Yeh couldn't wait to get up here and tell them, could yeh?

BEN: I didn't mean anything by it.

WILL: Did yeh not? Yeh still had to say it all the same. Yeh don't hear me up here telling them all that you like to slip into the bathroom and have a wank as soon as you think I'm asleep.

[They all look at BEN.]

BEN: *[in a panic]* Brushing my teeth! That's all, just brushing my teeth.

TINA: He meant no harm, Will.

WILL: Don't you talk to me either, yeh cheap brasser.

[In the background we hear EMILY singing "There's a Bright Golden Haze on the Meadow" in the shower. WILL walks to the door.]

WILL: And her, that loser. She should be singing "Old Man River". Her husband didn't send her here to improve her self-esteem, he sent her here to get rid of her for a few weeks.

BILL: *[in Perry Mason]* I must object here, your honour. This is purely speculation, and I want that on the record!

[WILL lunges at BILL.]

WILL: You fuckin' lunatic!

[There follows a skirmish on the bed. TONY stops it with a scream.]

TONY: Stop! Stop it now, all of you, you selfish shower of bastards.

[Everybody stops suddenly and turns in shock to TONY, amazed at his uncharacteristic outburst.]

TONY: What about Joe Daly and the trouble he's in?

[The melée breaks up and things calm down a little.
Everyone stands in silence, hanging their heads. Suddenly the bathroom door is flung open and out steps EMILY still drunk but now wearing fishnet stockings, suspender belt, red knickers and red bra.]

EMILY: *[singing]* "Do yeh think I'm sexy?
Do yeh want my body?
Come on, baby, let me know."

[EMILY freezes as she realises everybody in the room is staring at her. She gives a little yelp and disappears back into the bathroom where she slams the door.]

BEN: What in the name of Jesus was that?

[TINA jumps up.]

TINA: God, she's embarrassed. I should have told her you were here.

[TINA goes to the bathroom door, raps on it gently and calls.]

TINA: Emily, it's just me – Tina. I'm coming in.

[TINA enters the bathroom and closes the door. All four men burst out laughing. When the laughter has died down Will speaks up.]

WILL: Tony, what did you mean that time?

TONY: What?

WILL: When you said "selfish bastards", none of us thinking of Joe Daly. What did you mean by that?

TONY: Oh, well, I overheard a conversation, maybe I shouldn't say ... No, I will say. Mr Rubenstein is here to check up on Joe Daly and unless Joe Daly gets a seventy percent success rate from this class he's out of a job!

BEN: What's seventy percent of six?

WILL: Four, I think.

BILL: No, that's sixty-six percent. It has to be at least five.

[TONY sits on the bed slowly.]

TONY: Five of us must pass this course or Joe loses

his job, good grief.

BILL: *[in Peter Lorre voice]* Oh dearie me, they're making a big mistake. It was the hand, Rick, tell them it was the hand. *[sits]*

[BEN leans against the wall.]

BEN: Imagine having all your hopes pinned on six losers like us.

[The girls re-enter the room, gingerly in the case of EMILY. TINA takes in the faces.]

TINA: Now what's up?

TONY: I was just telling the lads I overheard a conversation: unless Joe Daly gets a seventy percent pass rate in this class he's out of a job. That means five of us have to pass.

[The two girls sit, EMILY now back to life.]

EMILY: Oh dear, poor Joe and such a nice man.

TINA: That's not fair. Why this class of all classes? We have to be the worst he's ever had.

[There follows a moment's silence. Then WILL speaks.]

WILL: Wait a minute, we're not losers, at least we don't have to be. Remember the principle of PMA: "We can all be what we want to be". We're not thicks, we've all taken something in. Bill, what are the three ingredients of sales enthusiasm?

BILL: Enthusiasm, Need and the Carolina Nod.

WILL: Correct! Tina, why is our PAP more beneficial to children then any other PAP?

TINA: Because we cover the children fully and even though they do not have an income of their own we pay them a full rate.

[WILL *turns as if to ask* TONY, *skips him and goes on to* BEN. TONY *is disappointed.*]

WILL: Ben, what's the opening statement after knocking at the client's door?

BEN: Good morning, Mr O'Brien, I've just been in with Mr Connolly next door and ... and ...

WILL: Come on, Ben.

BEN: And I believe I have something here which will interest you!

WILL: Yes! Emily what's the rebuttal to "I already have plenty of insurance?"

EMILY: You're so right to be concerned about the future of yourself and your family and we find that it's people who have lots of insurance who can readily see the benefits of our PAP which looks after the *immediate* needs in case of emergency. Now let me show you what I mean ...

[Everyone claps.]

TONY: This is great. We can teach each other.

WILL: That's right, Tony, yes, we can ... and you were also right about another thing: we can only do it if we stop thinking about ourselves and start working for each other and Joe Daly!

BEN: We've got six days to send that bastard Rubenstein packing. By Jesus, I'll give it me best shot: no more wank ... brushing me teeth for me. I mean business!!

EMILY: I'll help Tina with her rebuttals and anybody else who needs help.

WILL: And I'll ... and I'll try and stay off the drink. It's not a problem or anything, but I, I won't have any anyway.

[BILL walks to WILL and puts his hand on his shoulder.]

BILL: And, Will, I will try and not antagonise you any more.

[WILL puts his arm around BILL's waist.]

WILL: Thanks.

BILL: *[winks and adds.]* Here's looking at you, sweetheart!

[The two men laugh. The stage goes dark and one

minute of pre-recorded babble of learning murmurs plays over the tune of "It's a Long Way to Tippe-rary".]

Scene Three

[*The classroom next day. Slide 8 reads: "Burt Takes Over ... Or Does He?" The room is empty except for* JOE *and* BURT. *They are awaiting the arrival of the pupils.* BURT *is visibly excited, anticipating taking over the class for the day.*]

JOE: Are you sure this is wise, Burt?

BURT: I *know* this is wise, Joe. I have seen one week of your course and you still fail to inject any confidence into these people. Without confidence there's no PMA, without PMA there's no sales and that's the bottom line, Joe.

JOE: Well, if you're going to do this I should really leave.

BURT: No, Joe, you stay. Perhaps you might learn something too. Something you can take to your next position with you. Now show me in this manual how far you've gotten.

[The pupils now arrive with a look of determination on their faces. At least, five of them arrive: WILL is missing. They all take their seats. JOE stares for a moment. He knows there is something different about them.]

JOE: Good morning, everybody. We'll begin in just one moment.

[He returns to the manual to consult silently with BURT.]

TINA: Ben, where's Will?

BEN: I don't know. When I woke up this morning his bed was empty.

TONY: I hope he hasn't deserted us.

[The door opens and WILL walks in. He is dressed in a two-piece navy suit. His hair is brushed and gelled back. He is clean-shaven. He looks like a movie star. With a smile WILL takes his seat.]

WILL: Morning, everybody.

EVERYBODY: Hello, Will.

WILL: Good morning, Emily.

EMILY: Hello, William.

[JOE leaves BURT and sits by the flip chart. BURT smiles to the class.]

BURT: Good morning, everybody. Ok, let's begin.

[All stand and begin singing "It's a Long Way to Tipperary". BURT interrupts them.]

BURT: No, no, no. We'll dispense with that this morning.

[Everybody sits.]

BURT: I've been watching this class for the past six days and frankly it's not working, is it? I've been trying to discover what it is that's lacking in the course and over the last couple of days I've realised it's confidence. You guys don't have any confidence. Look at you, you're a bunch of losers.

[TINA raises her hand towards JOE.]

JOE: Eh, yes, Tina?

TINA: Joe, is this a test to see if we knock the bollix out of him, because I'm about to fail if it is.

[JOE stands and moves to the table.]

JOE: Eh, no, everybody, this is not a test. Mr Rubenstein partook some years ago in a course very similar to this one except he did it in the United States of America where the lecturers are much more ... direct. He's taking over the class for part of, well, if not all of, the day in an effort to try a little experiment. Just go along and you'll find that everything will be ok. Isn't that right, Mr Rubenstein?

BURT: That's more or less right, Joe, and I don't need you to explain my motives. And, eh, you, Tina, is it? In future for the rest of this day you will address your questions to me. I'm not playing softball here: if you can't stand the heat get out of the kitchen. I mean business. Anybody that doesn't mean business gather your gear and take a hike.

[TINA *stands and begins to gather her things.*]

TINA: I don't need this shit.

WILL: Tina ... no.

TINA: I won't be talked to like I'm dirt.

WILL: Tina, winners don't quit. Four more days.

[JOE *jumps up and walks to* WILL *staring at him in disbelief.* TINA *takes her seat.*]

BURT: Good. Now that I have your attention let me talk about confidence. When you walk in that door to make that sale, PMA will help you to make the sale. But it takes confidence to walk in the door. Sometimes only persistence will get you that sale, but only confidence will give you that persistence. I stand at that door and I say "Good morning, Mr O'Brien. I've just been with Mr Connolly next door and I believe that I have something here that will interest you." I say "for only forty-seven pence a week should any accident whatsoever require overnight confinement in a hospital, we pay one of the highest incomes ever paid in proportion to the premium. Or, if you wish to, you can do as most people do and for only ninety-four pence a week take the full unit and receive, while in hospital, two hundred and eighty pounds a week. Just think of it. Now here is something you will find in very few policies sold at this low cost: Following hospitalisation, there is usually a recovery period and should that happen we will continue to pay you at home for up to the same number of days as you are in hospital at a rate of one hundred and forty pounds per week. Should you lose your life, sight or limbs we pay up to six thousand pounds in a lump sum. Just think of that." I can make that pitch because I have confidence, you guys don't have it.

[TONY stands.]

TONY: For only forty-seven pence a week should any accident whatsoever require overnight confinement in a hospital, we pay one of the highest incomes ever paid in proportion to the premium. Or if you wish to, you can do as most people do and for only ninety-four pence a week take the full unit and receive, while in hospital, two hundred and eighty pounds a week beginning with the very first day and even for the rest of your life if necessary. Just think of it. Now here is something you will find in very few policies sold at this low cost. Following hospitalisation, there is usually a recovery period and should that happen we will continue to pay you at home for up to the same number of days as you are in hospital at a rate of one hundred and forty pounds per week. Just fucking think of that!

[TONY sits. BURT is stunned into silence momentarily.]

BURT: That's very impressive, Tony. Except you've had six days to learn that. Confidence is about reacting spontaneously.

WILL: I thought that was spontaneous enough, Mr Rubenstein. What is it you expect from people with confidence?

BURT: The confidence to do whatever it takes at a drop of a hat.

WILL: For instance?

[BURT walks to the table and points to TINA.]

BURT: You recite a poem, any poem.

[TINA stares with a frozen expression. BURT holds her stare for a couple of moments and then turns back to WILL.]

BURT: See ...

TINA: You are a child of the universe. No less than the birds in the trees you have a right to be free and whether or not it is clear to you, no doubt the universe is unfolding as it should.

[WILL gestures with his arm.]

WILL: See?

[BURT walks to BEN.]

BURT: You, tell a joke.

[BEN stands.]

BEN: Once upon a time there was two Chinese. Now look how many there is.

[All laugh.]

EMILY: There doesn't seem to be any lack of confidence here, Mr Rubenstein.

[BURT is now getting perturbed.]

BURT: Ok, sing a song. Anybody! Sing a song.

[The class glance at each other and WILL stands. He begins to sing "Mack the Knife". At the end of WILL's song the class clap. BURT stands, glaring at them. JOE stands.]

JOE: Eh, Burt, could I see you over here for a moment?

[They go to a corner of the stage.]

JOE: I think you handled that awfully well, Burt.

BURT: What? Eh ... I, eh, what?

JOE: That was one of the finest posi sessions I've ever seen.

BURT: *[calming]* Do you think so, Joe? Why, thank you. I had them going for a minute though, hadn't I?

JOE: Absolutely.

[They turn back to the class.]

JOE: I think you will all agree that Mr Rubenstein gave a wonderful posi session this morning and I think for that he deserves a little round of applause.

[The class clap.]

BURT: Em, thank you. Eh, Joe, I think I'll go and get myself a coffee.

JOE: Well absolutely, Burt, and thank you for this morning.

[BURT makes his way to the door. As he gets there BILL calls after him.]

BILL: Eh, Mr Rubenstein.

BURT: Yes.

BILL: How's your PMA?

BURT: *[feebly]* Fantastic.

[Exit BURT.]

JOE: Tony, that was a most impressive sales pitch.

TONY: I'm glad he didn't go any further, that's all I knew.

[They all laugh.]

JOE: And, Will, a touch of the old cabaret singer there.

WILL: *[interrupting]* I sang yeh know, once, in Madison Square Garden.

JOE: Bill?!

WILL: Well, it was somebody's fuckin' garden.

[They all laugh again. The phone rings. JOE returns to his desk and picks up the receiver.]

JOE: Hello ... yes, that's right. Emily Beechmont? Just one second. Emily?

[EMILY looks at TINA and TINA looks back at her.]

EMILY: I'm not here. I'm not available.

JOE: I'm afraid Mrs Beechmont is not available, do try later, thank you. No fucking golf today. *[slams down phone]*

TINA: Now you're talkin'.

JOE: Well, I have to say I was most impressed with what I saw this morning, but as Tony correctly said he didn't know any more for the sales pitch. We've got four days to try and knock you guys into shape. let's get our heads down and get some work done.

FADE OUT

Music: brass section of "Mack the Knife".

Scene Four

[Bedroom. Slide 9 reads: "Emily Gets an Injection of PMA." EMILY and WILL are going over the sales pitch.]

EMILY: Ok, Will, let's try them again. Which is the most crucial time in a sale?

WILL: A sale is made or lost within the first thirty seconds. That's not the nightdress you were wearing the other night, is it?

EMILY: Em, no, I was wearing an older one. This is one that I bought down town with Tina. Now, what's the most effective point in a sale?

WILL: Every sales person knows that it's absolutely crucial that a proper introduction is used. It looks really good on you.

EMILY: Thank you, Will, it feels good too. Now how important is attention? You looked wonderful when you walked into the class this morning.

WILL: Thanks, I haven't felt that good in years. Em, a sale will not be made unless your prospect is willing to listen. Was that your gear you were wearing the other night?

EMILY: Oh no, that belonged to Tina. How should we never address somebody in their work place? But I did buy some just like Tina's today.

WILL: We should never ask "Do you work here?" Instead even go so far as to ask "Are you the manager?" You were right to buy it, it looked great on you the other night.

EMILY: *[flustered]* Thank you, Will ... What is your most powerful tool?

WILL: What?

EMILY: A salesman. A salesman's most powerful tool.

WILL: Oh, the compelling force of the eyes. When held eye to eye *[WILL moves closer to EMILY]* a prospect can be taken in any direction.

> *[They stare at each other and come close as if to kiss. Suddenly the door begins to open and they move apart quickly. Enter TINA, BEN and BILL. TINA suspects what has been going on.]*

BEN: Hello. Be God you two look like you were hard at it.

EMILY: No ... no we were just, em going over some of the sales hints, weren't we, Will?

WILL: Yes, that's all, I mean that's right.

BEN: That's what I meant!

BILL: We're going over our rebuttals and we're not leaving this bedroom till we have them perfect. Would you care to join in?

[WILL *begins to leave.*]

WILL: Eh no, I'm going to work on my sales tips. It's ok, I'll go into my own bedroom next door. I know my rebuttals fairly well, I think.

TINA: Well, Emily, you know your rebuttals too, don't you?

EMILY: Reasonably well.

TINA: Come on, Emily, you're the best at them, so why don't you go in and help Will with his, em, tips.

EMILY: Will would probably prefer to learn alone, wouldn't you, Will?

WILL: Well, I wouldn't mind a bit of help.

EMILY: Well, ok, well, I'll, eh, just stick some clothes on me.

TINA: Ah, you're all right like that. Go on, it's only next door. Nobody will see yeh.

[Exit WILL and EMILY.]

BEN: Jesus, Will looked very red in the face. I hope he hasn't been drinking.

TINA: I don't think so.

BILL: Speaking of drink, I wouldn't mind a little nip myself.

[TINA produces a bottle of vodka and a large bottle of Coke.]

TINA: Ta-rah! I'll rinse out some glasses.

BILL: I'll get some ice from the machine on the landing.

[Exit BILL. TINA goes into the bathroom. BEN is lying on the bed. He picks up an empty glass on the bedside locker.]

BEN: Tina, there's a glass out here if you want another one.

TINA: No, it's ok. I have three.

[BEN toys with the glass for a moment then puts it to the wall and puts his ear to the end of the glass. After a couple of moments he cries out.]

BEN: Sweet Jesus. Tina!

[Enter TINA.]

TINA: What?

BEN: Oh, I think we're in trouble.

TINA: Why?

BEN: I think Will is gone off the deep end. I was right: he's been drinking, he's going to beat Emily up. We should call the guards.

[Enter BILL.]

BILL: Here we are. What's wrong?

BEN: Shush, shush, quiet 'till I tell yeh. I just heard Emily yelping and she going on about Will with a weapon.

[BILL and TINA laugh.]

BILL: It couldn't be ...?

TINA: It could ...

BEN: *[comes away from the wall]* Who's Roger Ramjet?

[TINA alone laughs.]

TINA: *[aloud]* Good girl, Emily.

FADE OUT

ACT THREE

Scene One

[*With the stage dark, Slide 10 reads: "Last Day, the Final Exam." When the stage is lit the six pupils can be seen bent over their exam papers. The clock is ticking in the background. BURT is sitting beside the flip chart and JOE is pacing nervously up and down. JOE walks to BURT.*]

JOE: How long is left?

BURT: Oh, just a couple of minutes.

JOE: Perhaps I could have a word with you, Mr Rubenstein.

[*BURT stands and brushes his suit down.*]

BURT: Well, make it snappy, Joe. I really do mean just a couple of minutes.

[*The two leave the room. Outside JOE speaks earnestly to BURT.*]

BURT: So what's your problem, Joe?

JOE: Burt, I just wanted you to know two things. Firstly in the five years that I have worked for the company I have to say that I was proud to be teaching their representatives in the field. I regard the company as one of the most honest and forward-thinking companies I have ever worked for. Whether you believe it or not, I really have given my best to every class of pupils I have ever taken in here. Regardless of how this class finishes with the results, I am proud to be a servant of the company.

BURT: They're all beautiful words, Joe. Now what was the second thing?

JOE: You're a prick!

BURT: Joe, what you think of me is irrelevant. I too like this company and I won't accept shoddy standards. I'm going to go in there and collect those exam papers. It'll take me just a few minutes to mark them up. I'll seal each result and I'll get the desk clerk to bring them back up to you. Then I'm off for a relaxing weekend, Joe, during which you will not cross my mind for one moment, believe it or not! However, when those results are opened if you do not have at least five of the six passed and ready to go into the field *according to my judgement*, on Monday morning I expect to have your resignation on my desk.

[BURT *looks at his watch.*]

BURT: And now, Joe, time is up!

[*The two men re-enter the room.*]

JOE: Time is up, everybody. Pens down if you please. Would you please fold your sheet in half and Mr Rubenstein will gather them.

[BURT *gathers the sheets and exits. Takes the lift.*]

JOE: Well, that's it, it's all over now. And you know something? The results really don't matter. What I mean is, how you did in that exam paper is not important to me. I just hope that each one of you leaves here after the last two weeks in some way a better person than you did when you entered.

[TINA *raises her hand.*]

JOE: Yes, Tina.

TINA: Joe, I wanna tell yeh this. I walked in that door two weeks ago with the hope in my heart that I would never have to ... well, yeh know ... again! And I want you to know this, Joe Daly: I gave that exam my best shot. I don't know if I did enough to pass, I don't think so, but even if I haven't passed and don't get this job, some day, somewhere in some office Tina Clarke will be doing somebody's business and when that day comes, Joe Daly, you'll be responsible.

JOE: No, Tina, you'll be responsible. You see, PMA really does work – just look what it's done for you.

[JOE turns and glances around the room. He points to BEN.]

JOE: Ben, what has PMA done for you?

[BEN stands confidently.]

BEN: It's taught me not to confuse education with intelligence. I may not be the best-educated man in the world, but I have enough intelligence to know that I am unique, I have drive and, by God, I have value.

[Everybody claps.]

JOE: Well done, Ben. Now, let me see.

[The phone rings. JOE walks to the phone and picks it up.]

JOE: Hello ... yes, just one minute.

[He turns to EMILY.]

JOE: Emily, it's for you. It's Bernard.

[EMILY rises, strides to the phone and picks the receiver up.]

EMILY: Hello, Bernard. I'm in the middle of a meeting now ... Bernard, you snivelling little shit, I said I'm busy. I'll try and call you later.

[*EMILY slams the phone down and walks back to her seat. Everybody claps.*]

JOE: Well, Emily, I don't have to ask you what PMA has done for you.

[*EMILY places her hand on TINA's hand.*]

EMILY: PMA. And Tina Clarke.

TINA: Thank you, Emily.

JOE: Anyone else?

[*JOE glances around the room. TONY slowly rises.*]

JOE: Tony?

TONY: I've learned that there has always been somebody controlling my life: my mother, my boss, my wife, and even my kids. Regardless of my results in this exam, when I walk out that door there will be one man in control: Tony Short.

[*Again everyone claps.*]

JOE: Anyone else?

[*Slowly WILL stands. All eyes turn to WILL.*]

WILL: I ... I used to ... *[he takes a deep breath. His eyes are filling.]* My name is Will Benson and I'm an alcoholic.

[WILL slowly takes his seat. There is silence for a moment then everyone claps. JOE crosses the room to WILL and extends his hand. They shake.]

JOE: Well done, Will Benson, well done.

[There is a knock at the door. All heads turn to look at it. JOE goes to it and opens it.]

VOICE OFFSTAGE: Message for Joe Daly!

[JOE takes the six envelopes and closes the door. He stands staring at them for a moment.]

JOE: It's the results.

[As JOE reads the names on the envelopes, he hands each person theirs. Nobody opens them. They all hold their envelope in their hand and stare at it.]

JOE: Well, come on. Somebody start, for God's sake!

[WILL begins to tear open his envelope. He takes out the folded piece of paper and reads what's on it. Slowly his eyes rise to meet JOE's.]

WILL: I passed it.

TONY: [*hungrily opens his and quickly says*] Pass!

[*For a moment no one moves. BILL stands up gallantly.*]

BILL: There can be no secrets in this man's army. A man's got to do what a man's got to do.

[*BILL whips open the envelope, extracts the paper triumphantly and reads.*]

BILL: Merciful Jesus, Joe. I've failed.

[*BILL leaves the paper on the table. Heads are bowed. He tries to speak to JOE then turns and leaves the room. TINA and EMILY open theirs simultaneously. They extract the piece of paper and EMILY speaks.*]

EMILY: No, wait, Tina! You read mine and I'll read yours.

[*They swap papers and unfold them simultaneously.*]

TINA: [*nervously to EMILY*] You passed, Emily. You passed!

EMILY: So did you, Tina!

[*The two hug and the men in the room clap. Suddenly all attention is focused on BEN. He slowly opens the envelope, unfolds the piece of paper and jumps from the table.*]

BEN: Pass! Sweet Jesus, pass! I passed, I passed ... oh good Lord, I passed. I passed.

[He runs to JOE and gives him a big hug.]

BEN: I passed.

JOE: Of course, you did, Ben. I knew you would.

WILL: That's five out of six. That's the seventy percent.

[WILL stands and walks to JOE.]

WILL: Congratulations, Mr Daly.

JOE: Thank you all very much.

[TONY now joining the three.]

TONY: No, thank *you*, Mr Daly.

JOE: Well, this calls for a real "posi" session.

[A piano arrives from side stage.]

JOE: *[tongue in cheek]* Oh look! There's a piano.

[JOE walks to the piano, lifts the lid and begins to play slowly. He sings what will be the chorus of the finishing song.]

JOE: Did you believe it?

That they'd still be here

On graduation day.

Now they are doers,

Now they are winners,

They have a part to play.

Into the business world they go,

Taking it day by day,

Never in doubt as to what they can do

With their PMA!

[The music shifts to marching tempo and the ensemble join in the chorus.]

GROUP:Who would believe that we'd still be here

On graduation day?

Now we are doers,

Now we are winners,

We have a part to play.

Into the business world we go,

Taking it day by day,

Never in doubt as to what we can do

With our PMA!

[Out of chorus, vamping it up, comes TINA.*]*

TINA: *[spoken]* I came here fourteen days ago

From working on the street.

Determined to make my future living

Standing on my feet.

I've never stuck with anything,

My life has been a sham.

But PMA has worked for me,

And to prove it here I am!

[Chorus.]

EMILY: *[spoken]* I came to do this course because

Bernard said I should.

He said I was lazy, fat and generally no good.

I wanted to improve my self-esteem,

Just a little bit.

Now thanks to PMA I know

Bernard is just a shit!

TONY: *[spoken]* I went to work every day

For twenty bloody years.

Familiarity can be okay,

But it fills you full of fears.

Don't take risks, toe the line,

Never go on strike.

But PMA has shown me

I can be anything I like!

[*Chorus.*]

BEN: [*spoken*] In school they called me slow,

Said I would never amount to much.

I grew up believing them,

With ne'er a dream upon which to clutch.

Then I walked into this room,

To find five people just like me.

By Jesus, I'm as good as any man,

You just wait and fuckin' see!

WILL: [*spoken*] Drink itself is not bad,

It's the man who holds the glass.

To think you can't control something

Sets you on your arse.

But PMA has taught me

Not to fear spirits or wine.

I can control them, if I want to,

And I will, one day at a time!

[*Chorus.*]

[BILL *has re-entered the room and the music slows to a love theme speed. All faces turn to* BILL: *they are sad.*
BILL *steps forward.*]

125

BILL: *[Spoken]* Life for me is on the screen,

It always has been, I'm afraid.

Of all of you on this course, I never thought

I would be the one to fail.

But I've learned that turning a negi to a posi,

Really is the key.

So fuck this selling insurance,

It's an actor's life for me!

[Chorus twice.]

FADE TO BLACK.

THE END

OTHER BOOKS BY
BRENDAN O'CARROLL
published by The O'Brien Press

*The best-selling, hilarious
Mrs Browne trilogy*

The Mammy

Agnes Browne is a strong woman – strong enough to cope
with widowhood, seven children, a tenement flat and the daily
grind of her Moore Street stall. But even strong women need a
little help and a dream of their own to keep them going ...

Over seven months in the Bestseller List

'a born storyteller'
THE LONDON INDEPENDENT

'Roddy Doyle had better watch out!'
THE CONNACHT TRIBUNE

*'Shades of O'Casey here, as well as Brendan Behan. A story as
colourful as Moore Street itself, but there is also
pathos, compassion and irony'*
ENTERTAINER

'full of devastating wit'
BOOKS IRELAND

The Chisellers

Three years after Redser's death Agnes Browne soldiers on, being mother, father and referee to her family of seven. Helped out financially by her eldest, and hormonally by the amorous Pierre, Agnes copes with tragedy, success and relocation to the 'wilds of the country' – suburban Finglas. And when an unscrupulous gangster threatens the family's dreams he learns a costly lesson – don't mess with the children of Agnes Browne!

The Granny

Agnes, now forty-seven, a granny and happily widowed for thirteen years, watches over the changing fortunes of her family – marriage, prison, broken relationships, literary success. Then the family begins to fragment and it seems that not even their mother's iron will can bring them together again. But you can never write off Agnes Browne!

All books paperback, £5.99

THE MAMMY *Talking Book*

Brendan O'Carroll reads his bestselling book
as only he can read it.
Two tapes, approx running time 3 hours. £8.99